GRACE AWAKENS

A DAILY INVITATION TO RISE

JOANN ANDREWS

Paperback ISBN: 979-8-9940608-0-3

Hardback ISBN: 979-8-9940608-1-0

eBook ISBN: 979-8-9940608-2-7

Credits

Back Cover photo: © Aislinn Rehwinkel

Copyright © 2025 JoAnn Andrews, All rights reserved.

Publisher: Graceful Empowerment, LLC

Trademark: Grace Map™ is a trademark of Graceful Empowerment, LLC

Book Design by HMDPublishing.com

A Note from JoAnn

You didn't land here by accident.

Maybe you're moving through loss, a quiet unraveling, or the ache of knowing you've outgrown your current life—but aren't sure what's next. I know that place intimately.

Grace Awakens was born out of my own healing after deep personal loss. It's the guide I longed for when the world kept asking me to "be strong" while I was still learning how to breathe again.

This book is your sacred space to reconnect with yourself. Each daily page offers reflection, gentle guidance, and an invitation to come home to who you really are.

We journey season by season—Winter through Fall—because just like nature, your soul blooms in cycles. There is wisdom in your stillness. Power in your pause. And beauty in every messy, magnificent step.

I'm honored to walk this journey with you. You are not alone.

With love and purpose,

JoAnn

To Madeleine and Thomas—

You are the reason I rise.

Every word on these pages carries a whisper of my love for you. Your strength, your kindness, your curiosity, and your courage have shaped me as deeply as any season.

May you always know the beauty of your own becoming. May you never forget that grace lives within you—and that you are endlessly, immeasurably loved.

This book is for your hearts, your futures, and the quiet mornings when you need a reminder of who you are.

With all my love, always.

THE JOURNEY
AT A GLANCE

Grace Awakens is your 365-day soul-led invitation to rise with clarity and purpose.

You'll move through four transformational chapters—Winter, Spring, Summer, and Fall—each aligned with a theme of awakening:

The Four Seasons of Grace

Winter: Clearing and Centering

In Winter, you are invited to slow down and take sacred pause. This is the season of stillness and reflection—a time to release what no longer serves you and make space for clarity. You'll begin to quiet the noise, reset your nervous system, and rediscover your inner foundation.

Spring: Healing and Reclaiming

As the ground thaws, your soul begins to stir. Spring is where you gently heal, grieve what's been lost, and begin to reclaim pieces of yourself that you abandoned or forgot. This is a tender, empowering season of renewal.

Summer: Aligning and Expanding

Summer is the season of radiance. Here, you step into alignment with your purpose, your values, and your joy. You will be asked to expand beyond your comfort zone—fueled not by force, but by flow. This is where confidence blooms.

Fall: Embodying and Thriving

In Fall, you gather the wisdom of the year. This is the harvest—where you integrate your growth and fully embody who you've become. You thrive not because you have it all figured out, but because you are finally living in truth and trust.

Every week builds on the last. Every day includes a reflection and a prompt to deepen your awareness. By year's end, you'll not just feel more grounded—you'll be transformed.

WINTER

Clearing and Centering

Winter is the sacred beginning of your journey—a season not of action, but of awakening. Just as nature quiets beneath the surface, you are invited to pause, reflect, and reset. This is a time for letting go of what no longer serves you, creating space within, and grounding yourself in stillness.

In these early days of the year, you'll explore clarity through quiet. You'll gently release old patterns, declutter your thoughts and surroundings, and begin again with intention. Winter reminds you that rest is productive, and that your inner world must be nourished before anything external can flourish.

Let this season be an offering to your soul: a return to center, a rebalancing of energy, and a recommitment to your truth.

JANUARY

JANUARY

Grace Practice:
The Sacred Beginning

Each morning this month, speak a daily intention aloud:

*"Today, I will walk with grace and
choose what honors my peace."*

Write it down.

At month's end, gather the intentions and reflect:

What patterns are calling you into deeper alignment?

January 1

Begin Again

You don't have to wait for permission or a perfect plan.
Begin where you are—with open hands and a willing
heart. Let today be the gentle reset your soul has been
waiting for. There is no shame in starting over—only
strength.

Invitation:
What would it mean to begin again—without guilt or apology?

January 2

Stillness is Sacred

Busyness often masks pain. Stillness invites truth.
Today, instead of filling the silence, meet it. In quiet
moments, the deepest clarity can rise.

Invitation:
What am I afraid to hear in the quiet?

January 3

Your Environment Reflects Your Energy

Our surroundings hold energy. When we clear a
drawer, wipe a surface, or make the bed, we signal
to ourselves that we are worthy of order and peace.
Today, choose one space to clear with intention.

Invitation:
*What clutter in my life (physical or emotional)
is ready to be released?*

January 4

Let It Go

You can't take flight with arms full of what no longer belongs. Release isn't always dramatic—it can be soft, sacred, slow. Even a single deep breath can be a release.

Invitation:
*What's one thought, belief, or burden
I'm ready to set down today?*

January 5

You Are Not Behind

You are not late. You are not lost. You are becoming.
Rest in the truth that you are on time for your own
life.

Invitation:
Where do I need to offer myself grace instead of pressure?

January 6

Peace in Simplicity

There is power in simplifying—your calendar, your expectations, your inner dialogue. Today, choose one thing to say no to—and one thing to say yes to that nourishes you.

Invitation:
What would feel more peaceful if I allowed it to be simpler?

January 7

Honor the Clearing

The act of clearing isn't about loss—it's about devotion to what matters. The more space you create, the more clearly you hear your soul's call.

Invitation:
What can I let go of that will create space for what I truly want?

January 8

The Gift of Slowness

Slowness isn't stagnation—it's sacred. In a world addicted to urgency, your ability to slow down is a radical act of self-love. Breathe deeply. Move gently. Today, walk with intention.

Invitation:
Where in my life do I need to slow down?

January 9

Return to Your Breath

Your breath is the first place peace begins. It doesn't need words or effort—just attention. Inhale calm. Exhale everything you don't need.

Invitation:
What does my breath teach me about how I'm feeling?

January 10

Noise Isn't Clarity

When your mind is crowded with distractions, clarity can't find its way in. Today, choose one way to reduce noise—digital, mental, or emotional—and observe what arises in its place.

Invitation:
What noise have I normalized that I now choose to silence?

January 11

You Are Safe to Pause

Productivity is not your worth. You are allowed to rest, to reflect, and to do nothing but breathe and be. You are safe to pause.

Invitation:
What part of me needs permission to rest?

January 12

Come Back Home

Sometimes we wander from ourselves. We lose our
center chasing roles, responsibilities, or expectations.
Today, call your spirit home. Light a candle. Place your
hand on your heart. Return.

Invitation:
How can I come home to myself today?

January 13

Sacred Silence

There is healing in the spaces between words. Let your silence be a sanctuary, not something to fill. Let the world soften around you.

Invitation:
When was the last time I allowed silence to speak to me?

January 14

Anchored in Peace

When you find your still point, no storm can shake you. Anchor into your peace—not because life is easy, but because you choose alignment over chaos.

Invitation:
What grounds me when the world feels uncertain?

January 15

Quiet is a Teacher

The quiet isn't empty. It's full of whispers—of truth, of intuition, of your soul's desires. Today, resist the urge to fill the space. Trust that the answers you need may rise in the stillness.

Invitation:
What message is waiting for me in the quiet?

January 16

The Wisdom of Waiting

There is deep wisdom in waiting—not passive delay,
but sacred preparation. Trusting the process is an act of
courage and maturity. Honor what is not yet ready to
unfold.

Invitation:
What am I learning while I wait?

January 17

Honor Your Inner Voice

Your inner voice often speaks softly. Unlike fear, which yells, your intuition whispers. Today, be still enough to hear it. Then be bold enough to believe it.

Invitation:
What has my intuition been trying to tell me lately?

January 18

Embrace the Unknown

You don't have to know the whole path to take the next step. The unknown isn't a threat—it's a sacred invitation. Walk slowly. Stay open.

Invitation:
How can I loosen my grip on needing to know?

January 19

Choose Trust Over Control

Control can feel safe, but it often blocks flow. Trust
isn't weak—it's wise. Let go of the illusion that you
have to hold it all together.

Invitation:
Where am I ready to release control and lean into trust?

January 20

Listen Deeper

Sometimes we listen to respond—not to understand.
Today, practice deep listening—not just to others, but
to yourself, to your body, to your spirit.

Invitation:
What is my heart trying to say beneath the noise?

January 21

You Are Held

Even when you feel alone, you are held—by Spirit,
by love, by the earth beneath you. Trust that you are
supported in ways you may not yet see.

Invitation:
Where in my life can I soften and allow myself to be supported?

January 22

Resistance is Information

Resistance often shows up as procrastination,
avoidance, or fatigue. It's not failure—it's information.
Pay attention to what your resistance is trying to
protect.

Invitation:
What might my resistance be trying to tell me?

January 23

Let Yourself Be Moved

True transformation doesn't happen through force. It happens when we allow life to move us—from within. Be open to the soft nudge, the gentle invitation.

Invitation:
What gentle pull am I being asked to follow?

January 24

The Fear Beneath Control

We often grip tightly out of fear. But control is not safety—it's restriction. What if safety came from surrendering to flow instead?

Invitation:
What fear am I holding beneath my need for control?

January 25

Soften Your Edges

You don't have to power through everything. You can move forward with softness and still be strong. Let your edge be tenderness today.

Invitation:
What would it look like to soften around this resistance?

January 26

Permission to Feel

Sometimes we resist emotions because we think they'll break us. But emotions aren't enemies—they're messengers. Give yourself full permission to feel.

Invitation:
What emotion have I been resisting that wants to be heard?

January 27

Flow Where You're Led

When you stop resisting, you start flowing. Trust that where you are being led is fertile ground—even if it's unfamiliar.

Invitation:
What would happen if I stopped resisting and started flowing?

January 28

Release to Rise

Every act of release is an act of trust. Let go not to lose, but to make room for something higher. You rise when you release.

Invitation:
What am I willing to release in order to rise?

January 29

The Power of What's True

Truth is quiet but powerful. When you root in what's real for you—not what others expect—you begin to feel peace return. Truth aligns, even when it disrupts.

Invitation:
What truth am I ready to acknowledge?

January 30

Radical Honesty

Being honest with yourself is the first act of love. Let your honesty be the beginning of liberation—not judgment.

Invitation:
Where am I not being fully honest with myself?

January 31

Integrity is Alignment

When your actions match your values, you feel whole.
Integrity isn't perfection—it's alignment. Today, return
to the center of your values.

Invitation:
*Where in my life can I align more fully with what matters to
me?*

FEBRUARY

FEBRUARY

Grace Practice: Love as a Daily Choice

Write one note of love to yourself each day.
A sentence. A whisper. A truth.

Seal each note with:

"I am lovable. I am loving. I am love."

Store them in a box or journal.
On hard days, let your own love hold you.

February 1

You Are Worthy of Devotion

To hold yourself sacred is to treat yourself like something precious. You don't have to earn it. You already are. Begin today with reverence.

Invitation:
What does it look like to treat myself as sacred?

February 2

Make Space for You

Create space in your day, your home, your heart—for you. This is not selfish. This is survival. You are allowed to exist without explanation.

Invitation:
Where in my life can I carve space that honors me?

February 3

Boundaries are Blessings

Boundaries are how we honor both ourselves and others. A loving "no" is sometimes the deepest "yes" to your own peace.

Invitation:
Where do I need to set (or re-set) a loving boundary?

February 4

Tend to Your Inner Altar

Your soul has an altar. What you place on it—
thoughts, energy, rituals—shapes your experience.
Today, tend to your inner altar with love.

Invitation:
What do I need to place on my inner altar today?

February 5

Worth Without Productivity

You are not what you do. You are not what you achieve. You are worthy because you are. Full stop.

Invitation:
In what ways have I equated my worth with my productivity?

February 6

Sacred Doesn't Mean Perfect

To hold yourself sacred doesn't mean polished or
flawless. It means honest. It means whole. Let your
imperfections be your poetry.

Invitation:
What would change if I believed I was sacred exactly as I am?

February 7

Light Your Own Flame

Waiting for others to validate your glow dims
your light. Today, light your own flame. Bless your
reflection. Honor your voice.

Invitation:
What part of myself am I ready to honor without apology?

February 8

The Beauty of Duality

You are not only the light. You are also the dark—the shadow, the depth, the mystery. Today, honor all parts of your being. Wholeness begins with welcoming it all.

Invitation:
What part of me have I rejected that now deserves my compassion?

February 9

Your Darkness Has Wisdom

Your pain, your grief, your uncertainty—they've taught you resilience. Don't fear the dark seasons. Within them lie some of your greatest revelations.

Invitation:
What truth has the dark taught me that light could not?

February 10

Grace Doesn't Always Glow

Sometimes grace looks like tears. Sometimes it sounds like silence. Let today be free of performance. Let grace meet you where you truly are.

Invitation:
What does grace look like for me today?

February 11

Honor Your Shadows

Your shadows are not flaws. They are parts of you that once protected you. Today, thank them. Then gently choose a new path.

Invitation:
What shadow part of me is ready to be met with gratitude?

February 12

Shine Anyway

Even on the days when you feel heavy, dim, or doubtful—you can shine. Not perfectly. Not loudly. But truthfully. That is enough.

Invitation:
Where can I offer myself gentle light today?

February 13

The Light Within

Your light is not dependent on others seeing it. It exists because you do. Let your soul glow from within, whether anyone notices or not.

Invitation:
What lights me up from the inside out?

February 14

Love All of You

On this day of hearts, chocolates, and roses—
remember this: you are worthy of your own love. No
matter what. Every piece. Every layer.

Invitation:
How can I love myself more deeply today?

February 15

A New Season Awaits

As Winter nears its close, take inventory of your growth. You've cleared, centered, softened, and rooted. You are not who you were in January—and that is grace.

Invitation:
What parts of me have changed over the past few weeks?

February 16

Let the Past Be the Past

Honor what brought you here, but don't drag it with you. You are allowed to carry the lesson and leave the weight.

Invitation:
What am I finally ready to lay down and leave behind?

February 17

Trust the Stirring

You may feel the first flicker of Spring within. The desire to grow, to stretch, to become. Let the stirring happen. It means you're ready.

Invitation:
What new longing is rising within me?

February 18

You Are Stronger Now

Not because you pushed—but because you allowed.
You softened. You stayed. You rose. Recognize your
resilience.

Invitation:
Where have I shown strength this season?

February 19

Set a Sacred Intention

Before entering Spring, set a soul-aligned intention.
Not a goal. Not a to-do. A quiet commitment to your
becoming.

Invitation:
What sacred intention do I want to carry into the next season?

February 20

Your Foundation is Ready

Winter was for clearing, grounding, and healing. Now, you are ready to build something new. The foundation is within.

Invitation:
What truth will be my anchor moving forward?

February 21

Thank Your Winter Self

She did the work. She sat in the quiet. She listened.
Today, thank the version of you that chose to grow in
the dark. She is why you are ready.

Invitation:
*What do I want to say to the version of me who made it through
Winter?*

February 22

Speak from the Heart

Your voice matters—not just what you say, but how you say it, and what energy stands behind it. Today, speak from a place of truth, not performance.

Invitation:
Where have I been quiet that I now feel called to speak?

February 23

Stories You've Outgrown

We all carry outdated stories—about our worth, our place, our past. Today, choose one story and rewrite it with grace.

Invitation:
What story am I ready to stop believing?

February 24

The Power of No

"No" can be one of the most loving things you say—to yourself and to others. It clears space for what's true.

Invitation:
Where do I need to say "no" in order to reclaim my yes?

February 25

You Get to Choose Again

Healing doesn't mean erasing the past. It means reclaiming your ability to choose now. You are not bound to who you used to be.

Invitation:
What choice can I make today that supports who I'm becoming?

February 26

Remember Your Why

When things feel messy, come back to your why. Not the pressure or the plan—but the heartbeat behind it all.

Invitation:
What am I doing that reconnects me to my purpose?

February 27

Show Up As You

There is no version of you more powerful than the real one. Show up without the mask. You are enough without the performance.

Invitation:
What would it feel like to show up as my whole self?

February 28

Reclaim the Mirror

Look at yourself today with eyes of love. Let the mirror
reflect back not flaws—but fire. You are radiant.
Believe it.

Invitation:
What part of me needs to hear "you're beautiful" today?

MARCH

MARCH

Grace Practice: Grounded in Becoming

Each day this month, take a 5-minute "stillness walk." No phone. Just steps, breath, and observation.
Ask yourself silently:

What is awakening in me right now?

Let your answers rise like spring shoots—gentle, slow, and honest.

March 1

Tenderness is Power

Healing doesn't require grand gestures. It begins
with tenderness. Today, soften with yourself. Let
compassion be your medicine.

Invitation:
What would it feel like to treat my healing with tenderness?

March 2

Let It Hurt, Then Let It Heal

Avoiding pain doesn't erase it. Today, let yourself feel it fully—not to dwell, but to release. Healing begins when feeling is safe.

Invitation:
What have I been afraid to feel that might actually set me free?

March 3

You Are Not Your Wounds

What happened to you shaped you—but it does not define you. You are not your trauma. You are your response to it.

Invitation:
What identity am I ready to shed so I can heal?

March 4

Be Gentle with the Past

Your past self did the best she could with what she knew. Offer her grace today—not judgment.

Invitation:
What does my younger self most need to hear from me right now?

March 5

Grieve What Didn't Happen

Healing sometimes includes grieving what *never* was—a dream, a parent's love, a path you hoped for. It's okay to mourn it.

Invitation:
What unspoken loss needs permission to be grieved?

March 6

Healing is Nonlinear

Some days you rise. Some days you rest. Trust the spiral of healing—not a straight line, but a sacred return.

Invitation:
Where have I grown even if it doesn't look like progress?

March 7

Love is a Healer

Let yourself be loved—by others, by life, by you. Love is the balm that mends what logic never could.

Invitation:
What form of love do I most need to receive this week?

March 8

Joy is a Compass

Joy isn't a luxury. It's a guide. A spark that points you toward what's alive within. Follow it today—even in small ways.

Invitation:
What's one small thing that brings me joy I can say yes to today?

March 9

Rediscover Delight

When was the last time you laughed? Felt wonder?
Let yourself be surprised? Today, invite delight into
your day.

Invitation:
What used to delight me that I'd love to feel again?

March 10

Let Joy Coexist

Joy and pain can live together. You don't have to be
fully healed to laugh. Let joy visit your heart, even in
its mending.

Invitation:
*Where can I give myself permission to feel joy even in the midst
of uncertainty?*

March 11

Create Joy on Purpose

Don't wait for joy to find you—cultivate it. Light
a candle. Dance in the kitchen. Call a friend. Be
intentional.

Invitation:
What's one joyful thing I can do today on purpose?

March 12

The Joy of Enough

Joy blooms in contentment. Not in lack, not in striving, but in the sacredness of *enough*. Let that be your mantra.

Invitation:
What part of my life feels like "enough" today?

March 13

Joy as Resistance

In a world that profits from your dissatisfaction, joy is rebellion. Choose it loudly. Choose it daily.

Invitation:
How can I reclaim joy as my quiet revolution?

March 14

Remember How to Shine

You were never meant to shrink. Let joy remind
you how to take up space again—with grace, with
boldness, with light.

Invitation:
What part of me wants to shine more freely?

March 15

Trust Begins Within

Self-trust is the quiet confidence that says: "I've got me." It isn't perfection—it's presence. Begin again today with one small promise you will keep to yourself.

Invitation:
What promise can I make—and keep—to myself today?

March 16

Listening is Trust

When you listen to your body, your spirit, your needs—you build trust. Today, pause and listen before you act.

Invitation:
What is my body or spirit trying to tell me?

March 17

Forgive the Times You Abandoned Yourself

You don't have to carry shame for every time you didn't choose yourself. Forgiveness rebuilds trust.

Invitation:
Where have I abandoned myself, and how can I come back with love?

March 18

Be Your Own Advocate

You are allowed to speak up for what you need—even
from yourself. Advocate for your peace. Advocate for
your dreams.

Invitation:
What do I need to ask myself for today?

March 19

Celebrate Follow-Through

Every time you do what you say you'll do, your self-trust grows. Today, celebrate even the smallest follow-through.

Invitation:
What is something small I followed through on that deserves recognition?

SPRING

The Season of Emergence

Spring is not a rush—it is a holy stirring. Beneath the surface, life awakens. What was buried begins to breathe again. The sun stretches, and so do you.

This is the season to plant tender dreams and water them with patience. Let go of the urgency to bloom all at once. Instead, root deeply. Choose grace over pressure.

Allow your life to thaw slowly, trusting that even the smallest green shoot holds the promise of fullness. You are not behind. You are right on divine time.

March 20

Rewrite the Narrative

If your inner dialogue says you're flaky, unreliable, or undisciplined—rewrite it. You are becoming trustworthy to yourself.

Invitation:
What new narrative do I want to believe about myself?

March 21

Trust the Becoming

Even when you wobble, even when it's slow—you are becoming. Self-trust is a process, not a finish line.

Invitation:
Where am I already showing signs of deeper self-trust?

March 22

The Courage to Be Visible

It takes courage to stop hiding. To stand in your truth without shrinking. Today, allow one part of you to be visible—to yourself, and to someone else.

Invitation:
What part of me have I been hiding that wants to be seen?

March 23

Worth Beyond Validation

You are worthy, even when no one claps. Even when no one affirms. Let your validation come from within.

Invitation:
Where have I been waiting for permission to feel worthy?

March 24

Own Your Story

You get to decide how your story is told. Don't let shame write your narrative. Speak from strength. Speak from love.

Invitation:
What part of my story am I ready to reclaim?

March 25

Let Yourself Be Loved

Being seen includes being loved—not just despite
your flaws, but within them. Open your heart to being
received.

Invitation:
Where in my life am I resisting being loved as I am?

March 26

Remove the Mask

You don't have to pretend to be okay when you're not.
Let yourself be real today. Let someone witness the
truth.

Invitation:
What would it feel like to remove the mask and be authentic?

March 27

Show Up Unfiltered

Show up not how you *should* be—but how you *are*.
Unfiltered. Present. Whole. That is more than enough.

Invitation:
Where in my life can I show up more fully and honestly?

March 28

Let Your Light Be Seen

You don't have to dim to belong. The world needs your brilliance. Let your light speak louder than your fear.

Invitation:
What fear do I need to release so I can shine?

March 29

Listen for the Spark

Creativity often whispers. It shows up in longings, nudges, visions that won't leave you alone. Listen today.

Invitation:
What's been quietly calling for my creative attention?

March 30

Start Before You're Ready

You don't need a perfect plan—just a willing heart.
Begin messy. Begin small. Begin anyway.

Invitation:
What creative idea am I ready to start imperfectly?

March 31

Your Soul is a Creator

You were made to bring beauty into the world. To express, shape, birth something meaningful. Trust that sacred impulse.

Invitation:
What's something only I can create from my soul?

APRIL

APRIL

Grace Practice: Sacred Clearing

Choose one small space each day to declutter—a
drawer, a corner of your mind, a story you've
outgrown.

As you release, say:

*"Thank you for what you gave me.
I now release you with love."*

Let clearing become a form of prayer.

April 1

The Practice Over the Product

Let creation be your devotion, not your performance.
You don't have to monetize your joy. Let it be sacred
for its own sake.

Invitation:
How can I return to creating without pressure?

April 2

Let Inspiration Lead

Don't force it. Let it come. Trust the rhythm of
inspiration—and follow it when it flows.

Invitation:
What inspires me lately, and how can I make space for it?

April 3

Create for Healing

Art heals. Writing heals. Singing, painting, building—
it all opens portals to self-repair. Let it do its work.

Invitation:
What healing can I access through creativity today?

April 4

You Are the Art

You are not separate from your creation. Your life is the canvas. Your choices are the strokes. Paint boldly.

Invitation:
What part of my life feels like a masterpiece in progress?

April 5

Alignment Over Approval

Choose what feels right over what looks right.
Alignment is peace—even if others don't understand it.

Invitation:
Where in my life am I seeking approval instead of alignment?

April 6

Your Inner Compass

Your inner knowing is wise. Let it guide you today
without the noise of outside opinions.

Invitation:
What does my gut say—even if it's inconvenient?

April 7

Wholeness Feels Like Truth

When your actions match your values, you feel whole.
Today, close the gap between your truth and your
behavior.

Invitation:
What's one area of my life that's asking for more honesty?

April 8

Say Yes from the Soul

Let your yes be soul-led, not fear-led. You don't have to please everyone—just stay true to you.

Invitation:
Where do I need to say no so I can honor a deeper yes?

April 9

Trust the Discomfort

Sometimes alignment feels hard. That's okay. Let discomfort be a sign of growth—not a reason to quit.

Invitation:
What discomfort am I experiencing because I'm growing?

April 10

Clarity Through Action

You don't have to know the whole plan. Take the next step in truth and clarity will follow.

Invitation:
What small action can I take today that feels aligned?

April 11

You Get to Realign

Fell out of alignment? That's okay. Realign as many times as you need. It's grace, not failure.

Invitation:
Where do I need to course-correct with compassion?

April 12

You Are Capable of More Than You Know

Growth is often uncomfortable because it stretches our edges. Trust that your capacity is expanding with every step you take.

Invitation:
Where in my life am I ready to stretch into more?

April 13

Rest to Expand

You don't expand through exhaustion. You expand through rest. Build your capacity by giving your nervous system what it needs: gentleness.

Invitation:
What kind of rest do I need most today?

April 14

Stop Shrinking

Stop apologizing for taking up space. You are allowed
to speak up, show up, and shine—fully.

Invitation:
Where am I still shrinking that it's time to stand tall?

April 15

Practice Holding More

Growth means holding both discomfort and
possibility. Begin with something small: more
patience, more gratitude, more breath.

Invitation:
What emotion or opportunity am I learning to hold right now?

April 16

Learn Your Limits

Expansion also means learning your *real* limits—not the ones fear created. Test them gently. Honor them honestly.

Invitation:
What boundary would honor my growth today?

April 17

Capacity Through Compassion

You grow faster with kindness than criticism. Today, meet yourself with the grace that expands your ability to evolve.

Invitation:
Where do I need to offer myself more compassion in my growth?

April 18

Celebrate Your Stretch

Every stretch is a sign of life. Growth doesn't mean
perfection—it means *trying*. Celebrate yourself for
doing the work.

Invitation:
What stretch am I proud of, even if it's still in progress?

April 19

Becoming Is a Process

You are not behind. You're becoming, moment by moment. Let go of rushing. Embrace your pace.

Invitation:
What would it feel like to honor where I am right now?

April 20

Choose to Evolve

Growth isn't automatic—it's a choice. A daily devotion. What you choose today shapes who you become tomorrow.

Invitation:
What small choice today supports who I'm becoming?

April 21

Shed What Isn't You

You don't have to carry versions of yourself that no longer fit. Let them go with love. Make room for the real you.

Invitation:
What version of me am I ready to shed?

April 22

Your Identity is Yours to Define

You are not your roles. Not your resume. Not anyone's expectation. Define yourself by your soul, not your story.

Invitation:
Who am I when no one is watching?

April 23

Let Her Rise

That powerful, peaceful, radiant woman within you?
She's real. Let her rise today. Make choices that align
with her presence.

Invitation:
What would the woman I'm becoming do today?

April 24

Becoming Requires Grace

Some days will feel wobbly. That doesn't mean you're doing it wrong. Becoming requires grace, not grit.

Invitation:
Where can I soften and offer myself patience in this becoming?

April 25

You Are Becoming Her

Not someday—now. With every brave step, with every boundary, with every breath. She is already within you.

Invitation:
How am I already embodying the woman I long to be?

April 26

Love Doesn't Mean Losing Yourself

You can love deeply and still say no. Boundaries are
how love breathes—not how it breaks.

Invitation:
Where am I afraid that setting a boundary will take away love?

April 27

Boundaries are Bridges

A boundary isn't a wall—it's a bridge that shows others how to love you well. It's a pathway to healthy connection.

Invitation:
What relationship could be strengthened by clearer boundaries?

April 28

Say it with Kindness

You can say what's true without being harsh.
Boundaries rooted in kindness create more safety, not
less.

Invitation:
What boundary do I need to express clearly and kindly?

April 29

Boundaries Reclaim Energy

Where your energy leaks, your peace disappears.
Boundaries restore your vitality. Reclaim what's yours.

Invitation:
What part of my life needs stronger energetic boundaries?

April 30

You Teach People How to Treat You

How you allow others to treat you teaches them what's acceptable. Choose self-respect over silence.

Invitation:
Where have I allowed behavior that doesn't reflect my worth?

MAY

MAY

Grace Practice: Everyday Delight

Create a "delight altar" in your home. Each day, place a small object, flower, or written note that sparks joy. Visit it each morning. Say:

"I choose delight. I choose life. I choose beauty."

Let joy become your compass.

May 1

Guilt is Not a Guide

Guilt often arises when you break old patterns. Let it pass. Guilt isn't truth—it's a signal that something new is happening.

Invitation:
What boundary feels right, even if guilt follows?

May 2

Boundaries Make Space for Love

When you honor your limits, love flows more freely.
Boundaries don't push love away—they purify it.

Invitation:
What boundary could allow love to feel safer and more
authentic?

May 3

Rooted Confidence

Confidence isn't arrogance—it's remembering who you are. Root down into your truth today. Let that be your power.

Invitation:
What is one truth I know about myself that I can stand in today?

May 4

Walk Like You Belong

You don't have to earn your place. You belong in every room you enter—because you bring your whole self there.

Invitation:
Where have I been shrinking that I now choose to walk tall?

May 5

Confidence is Built, Not Found

You don't find confidence—you build it, action by action. Choose one thing today that reminds you of your strength.

Invitation:
What action helps me remember my power?

May 6

Your Energy Speaks

Before you say a word, your energy enters the room.
Today, carry the energy of worthiness and calm
knowing.

Invitation:
How can I shift my energy before I walk into the next moment?

May 7

Worth Doesn't Waver

No circumstance, mistake, or opinion can shake your worth. Confidence comes from knowing that truth deep in your bones.

Invitation:
What would change if I truly believed my worth was unshakable?

May 8

Confidence is Quiet

You don't need to be loud to be powerful. Confidence whispers, "I'm here, and I know who I am." Let that be enough.

Invitation:
Where can I embody quiet confidence today?

May 9

Carry Yourself with Grace

Graceful confidence honors both your power and your humanity. Walk through this world with both.

Invitation:
What does graceful confidence look and feel like for me?

May 10

You Are Worthy to Receive

Receiving doesn't make you weak. It makes you human. Open your heart to the support, love, and kindness that wants to meet you.

Invitation:
What am I being offered that I'm resisting receiving?

May 11

Guilt is Not Gratitude

You don't have to feel guilty for being supported.
Gratitude is enough. Let your receiving be sacred, not
shameful.

Invitation:
Where have I confused guilt with gratitude?

May 12

Let Yourself Be Helped

You don't have to carry it all alone. Let someone help
today. Let them in. Vulnerability is strength.

Invitation:
Who or what could support me right now if I let them?

May 13

Say Thank You, Not Sorry

Receiving with grace means accepting goodness
without apology. Try saying thank you instead of sorry
today.

Invitation:
What compliment or help can I receive today without deflection?

May 14

Receiving Heals

Letting yourself receive can heal old wounds of unworthiness. Each yes softens what thought it had to do it all.

Invitation:
What story about not being worthy to receive am I ready to rewrite?

May 15

You Deserve to Rest

Let rest be a gift you receive—not a reward you earn.
Today, allow your body and mind to exhale.

Invitation:
What kind of rest do I most need, and how can I receive it today?

May 16

Abundance is Allowed

You are allowed to have more than just enough. You are allowed to thrive. Let yourself receive abundance without shrinking.

Invitation:
What would it feel like to receive abundance with open hands?

May 17

Divine Timing

You are not late. You are not early. You are right on time. Trust that your life is unfolding with wisdom.

Invitation:
Where am I comparing my timing to someone else's?

May 18

Pause is Part of the Path

Just because it's not happening *now* doesn't mean it's not happening. Sometimes the pause is the preparation.

Invitation:
What is the pause teaching me?

May 19

Your Pace is Sacred

Rushing doesn't guarantee results. Slowness doesn't mean stuck. Honor your sacred pace today.

Invitation:
How would I move today if I trusted my natural pace?

May 20

Let Go of the Timeline

You don't have to force your life into a schedule.
Growth doesn't happen on a spreadsheet. Surrender
the false timeline.

Invitation:
What would it feel like to trust my timing instead of control it?

May 21

Delay is Not Denial

Just because something hasn't happened yet doesn't mean it won't. Delay is often divine protection or preparation.

Invitation:
What desire am I still holding onto with hope?

May 22

Timing Reveals Readiness

Sometimes what you want takes time because *you* need time. Trust that the version of you who will receive it is still unfolding.

Invitation:
How am I becoming the woman who is ready for what I desire?

May 23

Trust the Slow Bloom

A bloom cannot be rushed. Neither can you. Let your
life open in its own rhythm.

Invitation:
*What area of my life is blooming slowly, and how can I trust it
more deeply?*

May 24

Discipline with Delight

Discipline doesn't have to feel like punishment. When rooted in joy, it becomes devotion. Let your practices be loving, not rigid.

Invitation:
What would joyful discipline look like for me?

May 25

The Beauty of Consistency

You don't have to go hard—just go often. Gentle
consistency creates miracles over time.

Invitation:
What small act of consistency can I honor today?

May 26

Progress, Not Perfection

Perfection is the enemy of joy. Let your discipline be imperfect and alive. Show up as you are.

Invitation:
Where am I holding myself to unrealistic standards?

May 27

Motivation Follows Movement

Don't wait to feel ready. Move first—motivation will
meet you there. Begin, and let the fire follow.

Invitation:
What is one thing I can do today, even without motivation?

May 28

Return to Your Rhythm

If you've wandered, come back. You're not starting over—you're starting from experience. Let today be a return.

Invitation:
What rhythm am I ready to reclaim?

May 29

Align Your Habits with Your Heart

Let your daily actions reflect what you care about
most. Let discipline be an act of love.

Invitation:
What habit no longer aligns with my highest values?

May 30

Celebrate the Follow-Through

Following through on what you promised yourself is an act of self-respect. Celebrate even the tiniest win.

Invitation:
What did I follow through on this week that deserves celebration?

May 31

The Woman You're Becoming

She is not far away. She's within you now. Every brave
choice, every healed wound, every kind thought—she
grows.

Invitation:
What would it feel like to live today as if I already am her?

JUNE

JUNE

Grace Practice: Radiant Living

Each morning, step outside and turn your face toward
the sun. Say aloud:

"I am light. I am powerful. I am joy."

Feel the warmth fill your chest. Carry that energy into
your day—bold, open, radiant.

June 1

Growth Feels Like Stretching

Becoming isn't always graceful. It stretches. It aches.
But it also opens. Trust the stretch.

Invitation:
Where in my life am I stretching into a fuller version of myself?

June 2

Let Go of the Old Identity

You are not who you were. That's not failure—it's evolution. Let the old version of you rest.

Invitation:
What part of me is ready to be released with love?

June 3

Trust Your Becoming

There's no rush. You don't have to figure it all out.
Becoming is not a race—it's a rhythm. Stay with it.

Invitation:
What would trusting my process look like today?

June 4

The Quiet Shifts Matter

Transformation often happens in unseen ways.
Celebrate the small shifts. They build the foundation.

Invitation:
What quiet inner shift have I made that deserves recognition?

June 5

You Don't Have to Arrive

Life isn't a destination. You're allowed to be in progress. Becoming is living with open hands.

Invitation:
Where can I release the pressure to have it all together?

June 6

You Are Becoming Her

One breath at a time. One boundary at a time. One bold step at a time. You are already becoming her.

Invitation:
What is one thing I can do today to step deeper into her?

June 7

The Gift of Openness

Life flows to the open heart. The more you soften, the more you receive. Let go of resistance. Let life in.

Invitation:
What might life be trying to give me that I'm finally ready to receive?

June 8

A Birthday of Becoming

Today is more than a birthday. It's a sacred pause—a moment to honor the life you've lived, the woman you've become, and the dreams still unfolding inside you. You've walked through fire and still opened like a flower. You've built beauty from brokenness. You've chosen grace when grief made no sense. And today, the universe bows to your resilience. Let today be filled with love and abundance. Let joy wrap around you like sunlight. Let this next year be one where you stop asking permission to bloom. You are not just celebrating a birthday—you are celebrating a becoming.

Invitation:
What part of my journey deserves to be honored and celebrated today?

June 9

Stay Open When It's Uncomfortable

Sometimes openness feels vulnerable. But discomfort
is often the doorway to deep connection and growth.
Stay with it.

Invitation:
*What part of life am I being invited to open up to—even if it's
uncomfortable?*

June 10

Release the Timeline

You don't have to have it all figured out. Life has a
way of showing up when you show up. Release the
pressure. Receive the present.

Invitation:
What pressure can I release so I can receive today more fully?

June 11

Let Life Surprise You

Control is safe. Wonder is sacred. Today, let go of your plan and let something unexpected delight you.

Invitation:
How can I invite more magic into my day?

June 12

Welcome the Unknown

The unknown is where all possibility lives. Stay open to what's not yet clear. Let uncertainty be sacred.

Invitation:
What might be waiting for me in the space I've been afraid to explore?

June 13

Say Yes to Life

Say yes to love. Say yes to risk. Say yes to yourself. Let this be the week you say yes with your whole heart.

Invitation:
What is life inviting me to say yes to?

June 14

Surrender Isn't Giving Up

Surrender is choosing peace over control. It's trusting that the moment you're in is enough. Lay down the urgency today.

Invitation:
Where in my life am I trying to control what needs to be surrendered?

June 15

This Moment is Sacred

This breath, this hour, this step—it's all sacred. Don't miss it chasing what's next. Be here.

Invitation:
What beauty exists in this present moment that I haven't noticed?

June 16

The Gift of Presence

Presence allows us to feel more, love more, and need
less. Let it anchor you today.

Invitation:
How can I ground myself in presence when I feel overwhelmed?

June 17

Life is Happening Now

Not tomorrow. Not when the checklist is done. Not once you're "ready." Right now.

Invitation:
What joy can I choose in the now?

June 18

Let It Be Enough

What you've done today is enough. Who you are today
is enough. Let enoughness be your exhale.

Invitation:
Where have I been striving for more when peace lives in enough?

June 19

Receive This Moment

Don't rush past what's good. Receive the compliments.
Receive the sunrise. Receive yourself.

Invitation:
What part of today can I receive fully instead of rushing past it?

SUMMER

The Season of Radiance

Summer is your invitation to be seen. This is the season of full bloom—of vibrant life, creative fire, and embodied joy. The sun is high, and your soul is ready to rise with it.

Let this be your time of full presence—of sacred sweat, belly laughter, spontaneous beauty, and open-hearted courage.

But remember: radiance doesn't have to roar. You can glow without burning out. You can shine and still rest. Align your light with your truth, and let your life feel like sunlight.

June 20

Now is All We Ever Have

Make peace with the present. Let your life unfold from here—not fear.

Invitation:
What fear about the future can I release in order to live now?

June 21

Summer Begins – Shine Anyway

Today, the light stays longest. Let this be your reminder: you don't have to dim. You are allowed to take up space with your brilliance.

Invitation:
Where have I been dimming my light, and how can I shine freely today?

June 22

You Are the Sun

There's a fire in you that no one can extinguish. Let your warmth, your boldness, your power radiate outward.

Invitation:
What part of me is ready to be seen in full color?

June 23

Light Reveals

Summer's light reveals what's ready to bloom—and what needs to be released. Let clarity rise.

Invitation:
What truth is summer revealing to me?

June 24

Radiance Requires Rest

Even the sun sets. Let yourself radiate without burning
out. Rest is what keeps you glowing.

Invitation:
Where can I allow rest to fuel my radiance?

June 25

Confidence is Contagious

When you live with embodied confidence, others rise with you. Be bold in your joy. It gives others permission to do the same.

Invitation:
What would it feel like to live confidently and unapologetically today?

June 26

Stay Lit From Within

External validation fades. Internal fire lasts. Keep your glow sourced from your soul.

Invitation:
What keeps my inner light strong?

June 27

Let Your Radiance Lead

Let your life shine like a lighthouse—leading you and others back to truth.

Invitation:
How can my radiance serve something greater than me?

June 28

Joy is Your Birthright

Joy isn't a reward—it's a right. You don't have to earn it. Let yourself feel joy without needing a reason.

Invitation:
What joy am I ready to let in without justification?

June 29

Let Play Return

Play isn't childish—it's healing. Let yourself laugh,
move, create. Your soul craves lightness.

Invitation:
What playful practice have I been craving?

June 30

Joy Anchors You

When the world wobbles, joy can be your root. Not the fleeting kind, but the steady joy of being alive.

Invitation:
What does anchored joy feel like in my body?

JULY

JULY

Grace Practice: Permission to Rest

Pick one day each week to be a "Soul Sabbath." No errands. No tasks. Only what fills you—naps, nature, books, solitude, or laughter.

At the end of the day, write this:

"I am worthy of rest. My joy is sacred. My presence is enough."

Repeat weekly.

July 1

You Always Have a Choice

Even when it feels like you don't—there's always a
choice. A way to respond with grace. A way to return
to your power.

Invitation:
Where do I need to remember that I have a choice?

July 2

Choose What Serves

Every decision is an offering. Choose what nourishes
your peace, your joy, your growth.

Invitation:
What choice would best serve the woman I'm becoming?

July 3

Decision is a Sacred Act

To decide is to declare your worth. Let your yes mean yes, and your no mean no. Let it be holy.

Invitation:
What decision am I ready to make with courage?

July 4

Freedom in the Choice

Freedom isn't just external—it's internal. Choosing from your truth is the most liberating act there is.

Invitation:
What truth do I need to choose today, even if it scares me?

July 5

Compassion is a Daily Choice

You won't always get it right. You don't have to. Let
self-compassion be the practice that steadies you.

Invitation:
Where do I need to offer myself softness instead of shame?

July 6

Speak Kindly to Yourself

Your inner voice sets the tone for your life. Let it
sound like someone who loves you.

Invitation:
What's one kind thing I can say to myself today?

July 7

The Grace of Mistakes

Mistakes aren't failures—they're invitations to grow.
Let grace meet your humanity.

Invitation:
What mistake am I ready to forgive myself for?

July 8

Release the Inner Critic

That voice telling you you're behind, not enough, too much—thank it, then let it rest. It's time to lead with love.

Invitation:
How would I treat myself today if I replaced judgment with compassion?

July 9

Give Yourself What You Need

Sometimes self-compassion is a nap. Sometimes it's boundaries. Sometimes it's celebration. Listen in.

Invitation:
What do I truly need today, and how can I give it to myself?

July 10

Honor the Effort

You're doing more than you think. You're becoming in ways you can't always measure. Celebrate the effort.

Invitation:
What quiet effort deserves recognition today?

July 11

Be Your Own Safe Place

Come home to yourself. Let your heart be a sanctuary.
Let compassion be your anchor.

Invitation:
How can I offer myself safety and grace in this season?

July 12

Wholeness Over Perfection

You were never meant to be flawless. You were meant to be whole—real, complex, alive. Let that be enough.

Invitation:
Where can I embrace my wholeness instead of chasing perfection?

July 13

Let the Mess Be Sacred

Your mess tells a story. It reveals your humanity, your effort, your becoming. Let it be sacred—not shameful.

Invitation:
What part of my life looks messy but is actually a sign of growth?

July 14

Wholeness Welcomes Every Part

You don't need to cut off the "imperfect" parts to be worthy. Let them be held in the circle of your becoming.

Invitation:
What part of me needs love, not fixing?

July 15

Wholeness is Integration

It's not about fixing yourself—it's about integrating
every part. Wholeness says: all of me belongs.

Invitation:
How can I honor both the light and shadow in me today?

July 16

Give Grace to the Gaps

There will always be gaps—between who you are and
who you're becoming. Let grace fill them.

Invitation:
What gap in my life needs more grace than judgment?

July 17

Imperfect Progress is Still Progress

Progress doesn't have to look pretty. Let each step,
however messy, carry meaning.

Invitation:
Where have I made quiet progress that deserves celebration?

July 18

You Are Already Whole

There's nothing to earn. Nothing to prove. Right here,
right now, you are enough.

Invitation:
What would it feel like to live as if I am already whole?

July 19

Honor Your Cycles

Just like the moon, you're not meant to shine at
full strength every day. Today, listen to your body's
rhythm.

Invitation:
What is my energy trying to tell me today?

July 20

Rest is Not Laziness

Rest isn't weakness. It's wisdom. It's how your body
and spirit repair, integrate, and rise again.

Invitation:
How can I honor rest without guilt?

July 21

Make Space for Stillness

Stillness is not empty. It's sacred. In the quiet, your
inner voice becomes clear.

Invitation:
What clarity might arise if I give myself space to be still?

July 22

You're Allowed to Pause

You don't have to keep pushing. Give yourself
permission to pause—without apology.

Invitation:
Where in my life do I need a pause to reconnect with myself?

July 23

Rest as Resistance

In a world that glorifies hustle, rest is a radical act of self-respect. Let your rest be revolutionary.

Invitation:
How can I reclaim rest as an essential part of my power?

July 24

Align with Nature's Pace

Nature doesn't rush, yet everything blooms in time.
Let yourself align with a gentler, truer pace.

Invitation:
*What would change if I allowed myself to bloom on my own
timeline?*

July 25

Restore to Rise

You can't rise strong without restoring deeply. Let
today be about filling your cup.

Invitation:
What restores my spirit and how can I prioritize it?

July 26

Anchor into Your Truth

Let your truth ground you. No matter the wind, you can root yourself in who you really are.

Invitation:
What truth can I return to when life feels uncertain?

July 27

Strength in Stillness

Your strength doesn't always roar. Sometimes, it whispers. Let stillness be your anchor, not your weakness.

Invitation:
Where have I mistaken stillness for weakness?

July 28

Keep What Grounds You Close

When the noise gets loud, return to the rituals and people that bring you home to yourself.

Invitation:
What keeps me grounded—and how can I protect it?

July 29

Breathe Through the Storm

You don't have to fight every storm. Some are meant to pass. Let your breath carry you through it.

Invitation:
How can I soften and breathe through what I'm facing?

July 30

Root Before You Rise

Before rising high, root deep. Let your foundation be
steady. There is no rush.

Invitation:
What area of my life needs deeper roots before expansion?

July 31

Be the Calm in the Chaos

You are allowed to be calm even when the world is
not. Peace is your power.

Invitation:
How can I protect my peace in the midst of external chaos?

AUGUST

AUGUST

Grace Practice: Wholeness Without Perfection

Each day, name one "imperfect" thing about yourself
or your life—and say thank you for it.
Let it be a thread in your beautiful, whole tapestry.
End each note with:

"I see you. I love you. I'm proud of you."
Save them in a jar or journal to reread when needed.

August 1

Step Into the Light

It takes courage to be seen—to live unhidden. Today,
let yourself be visible in your truth.

Invitation:
*Where have I been hiding, and what part of me is ready to be
seen?*

August 2

Let Your Voice Be Heard

Your voice matters. Let it tremble if it must, but let it speak. Truth heals.

Invitation:
What truth do I need to give voice to today?

August 3

Vulnerability is Strength

Your softness is not a liability. It's the bravest thing
about you. Let your tenderness lead.

Invitation:
How can I allow vulnerability to open more connection?

August 4

You Don't Need to Be Perfect to Be Powerful

Authenticity carries more power than perfection ever could. Be real. Be whole.

Invitation:
What mask am I ready to release?

August 5

Reclaim Your Spotlight

There is a place in this world only you can fill. Stop shrinking. You were made to shine.

Invitation:
Where am I ready to reclaim my space?

August 6

Lead with Heart

Let your heart be your compass. Even in fear, even in doubt, trust the deeper knowing.

Invitation:
What would my heart do if it were leading today?

August 7

Be Fully Here

Don't withhold your presence. This life, this moment,
needs all of you.

Invitation:
What part of me have I been holding back?

August 8

Living Devoted

Let your life become your devotion. Every act—
brushing your hair, tending your home, walking in
nature—can be holy.

Invitation:
What simple ritual can I treat as sacred today?

August 9

Devotion is a Daily Practice

Devotion isn't in the grand gestures. It's in the quiet repetition. The willingness to return again and again.

Invitation:
What am I willing to return to—even when I don't feel like it?

August 10

Make Room for the Sacred

Sometimes devotion looks like removing the clutter—
of thought, schedule, or space. Make room for what
matters.

Invitation:
What do I need to clear to make space for what's sacred?

August 11

Let Love Be the Reason

Not pressure. Not performance. Let love fuel your
rituals, your work, your words.

Invitation:
What would shift if I moved from love instead of obligation?

August 12

Devotion Includes You

You are worthy of your own care. Your own reverence.
Let your attention return inward.

Invitation:
What would it look like to be lovingly devoted to myself?

August 13

Choose One Thing

Don't do it all. Just do one thing with presence. Let it
be your offering.

Invitation:
What one thing will I do today with full devotion?

August 14

Let It Be Enough

Whatever you do today—do it with heart, and let it be enough. That is devotion in its highest form.

Invitation:
Where can I stop striving and let my wholehearted effort be enough?

August 15

Reap What You've Planted

You've been sowing seeds all season—in healing, in love, in courage. Today, notice what is finally blooming.

Invitation:
What fruits of my effort can I celebrate today?

August 16

Tend to Your Inner Garden

Harvest is not only about reaping—it's about tending.
Keep nurturing what still needs care.

Invitation:
What part of me still needs tending before it fully blooms?

August 17

Honor the Invisible Work

Not all progress is visible. Some roots grow deep
underground. Trust the unseen harvest within.

Invitation:
What inner growth can I honor—even if no one else sees it?

August 18

Keep What Nourishes

Now is the time to harvest what truly feeds your soul.
Let the rest fall away.

Invitation:
What is truly nourishing me right now?

August 19

Celebrate the Season

Pause and look around. You've come far. Let this moment be a celebration of your brave becoming.

Invitation:
How can I honor and celebrate this season I've lived?

August 20

Share the Abundance

Harvest is meant to be shared. Let your joy, wisdom,
and love ripple outward.

Invitation:
What can I offer others from the abundance in my life?

August 21

Reflect Before You Replant

Before rushing into the next season, reflect. What
worked? What will I leave behind? What do I want
more of?

Invitation:
What lessons will I carry with me into the next season?

August 22

Transitions Are Sacred

Change is not a disruption—it's an invitation. Let this moment of transition hold your attention, not your resistance.

Invitation:
How can I treat this transition as sacred?

August 23

Let Go With Grace

What once served you may no longer fit. Release it gently. Bless
what's ending.

Invitation:
What am I ready to release with gratitude?

August 24

Hold the In-Between

You're not who you were, and not quite who you're becoming. That's okay. The in-between is fertile ground.

Invitation:
How can I offer myself compassion in the in-between?

August 25

Trust the Unknown

The unknown isn't empty—it's alive with possibility.
Let yourself be curious instead of afraid.

Invitation:
What would it feel like to greet the unknown with curiosity?

August 26

Rest Before the Rise

Like the earth before a new season, your soul needs
quiet before its next blooming. Rest without guilt.

Invitation:
Where can I pause to restore before rising again?

August 27

Honor What Was

Look back with kindness. Everything you've walked through shaped you. Honor it.

Invitation:
What part of my past do I want to honor before moving forward?

August 28

Choose Again

Each day is a chance to realign. Choose again. Choose what matters. Choose what's true.

Invitation:
What new choice am I being invited to make?

August 29

Breathe into What's Next

The future doesn't need to be figured out—it needs to be breathed into. Inhale trust. Exhale control.

Invitation:
What if I didn't need to plan, only to trust the next breath?

August 30

You Are Ready

You've done the work. You've lived the season. You are ready for what's next—even if it doesn't feel like it.

Invitation:
What evidence do I have that I'm ready for this next chapter?

August 31

Bless the Ending

Endings are beginnings in disguise. As you close this season, let it be with grace, celebration, and deep self-respect.

Invitation:
What blessing can I speak over this chapter of my life?

SEPTEMBER

SEPTEMBER

*Grace Practice: Honoring
Your Inner Compass*

Each morning, ask: *"What does my soul need today?"*

Write down the first answer without judgment. Follow it—
through a boundary, a rest, a risk, or a sacred no.

By month's end, notice how trust has deepened.

September 1

Begin Again—Rooted in Wisdom

You don't start over empty-handed. You carry the gold of what you've lived. Begin again, rooted in truth.

Invitation:
What inner wisdom am I bringing with me into September?

September 2

Let the Leaves Fall

Nature lets go without drama. Let the things no longer meant for you fall with grace.

Invitation:
What am I ready to release with peace?

September 3

Come Home to Yourself

Let September be a homecoming. No more running. No more performing. Just you, anchored and whole.

Invitation:
What does it mean to come home to myself this season?

September 4

Truth Sets You Free

Your truth will never betray you. Listen to it. Speak it.
Let it lead.

Invitation:
What truth have I been quieting that needs a voice?

September 5

Slow is Sacred

You don't have to rush your roots. Let slow be sacred.
Let it nourish you.

Invitation:
Where is life asking me to slow down and deepen?

September 6

Tend to What's Real

Strip away the noise. What remains is what's real. Tend
to that.

Invitation:
What truly matters to me right now?

September 7

Rest in What's True

Truth doesn't demand. It whispers. It holds. It roots
you. Rest in it.

Invitation:
What truth can I rest in today?

September 8

Alignment Feels Like Peace

You know when you're in alignment—not because it's easy, but because it feels honest. Follow that.

Invitation:
What part of my life feels most aligned—and how can I build on it?

September 9

Let Your Yes Be Yes

Don't say yes when your soul says no. Honor your
boundaries as sacred.

Invitation:
Where am I being called to honor a sacred no?

September 10

Your Values Are a Compass

Let your decisions reflect your values—not pressure or habit. That's how alignment becomes embodied.

Invitation:
What value do I want to embody more fully this week?

September 11

When It's Not Aligned, It Drains

If it depletes your joy or peace, it's worth questioning.
Alignment restores energy.

Invitation:
What's draining me that I may need to step away from?

September 12

Small Shifts Create Big Change

You don't have to blow up your life to get aligned.
Small shifts compound.

Invitation:
What one shift would bring me into greater alignment today?

September 13

Your Body Knows

Before your mind rationalizes, your body knows. Tune
in. Trust the wisdom within.

Invitation:
What is my body telling me about what's aligned or not?

September 14

Return to What's True

If you've wandered, come back. You're never too far
gone for alignment.

Invitation:
What truth do I need to return to this week?

September 15

Release Isn't Loss, It's Liberation

Letting go isn't losing—it's creating space. Trust that
what you release will return as peace.

Invitation:
What am I ready to let go of with love?

September 16

Grieve the Old

Even when it's right to release something, grieving is natural. Let it move through you gently.

Invitation:
What goodbye do I need to grieve to move forward?

September 17

What You Keep Should Keep You

What you hold onto should nourish you, not weigh
you down. Reassess what stays.

Invitation:
Is what I'm holding still holding me in return?

September 18

Release the Role

Sometimes what we release isn't a person or place—it's a version of ourselves. Thank her, then let her rest.

Invitation:
What role or identity am I outgrowing?

September 19

Make Room for What's New

Your next chapter is waiting for space. Let the clearing
be your sacred preparation.

Invitation:
What newness do I desire to invite in?

September 20

Let Go in Layers

You don't have to release it all at once. Let go in layers,
at your own pace.

Invitation:
What's one layer I'm ready to release today?

September 21

Peace Follows Release

Letting go may hurt—but it also heals. Peace follows
surrender.

Invitation:
What peace am I making space for through letting go?

FALL

Fall is the sacred homecoming. As the world quiets and leaves begin to fall, you are invited to return to yourself.

This is the season of harvest—of celebrating what has grown, honoring what must go, and gathering what will nourish you through the stillness ahead.

Let yourself reflect, release, and realign. Let fall remind you that letting go is not failure—it's wisdom.

You don't have to carry everything forward. You just have to carry what matters.

September 22

Anchor First, Then Rise

True elevation comes from grounded roots. Root into
your values before you reach higher.

Invitation:
What foundation do I need to strengthen before I expand?

September 23

The Autumn Equinox

Balance is sacred. Today, day and night are equal. Let this be your mirror—honoring both action and rest.

Invitation:
Where am I being called to create balance?

September 24

Rise in Your Season

You don't need to match someone else's pace. Rise in
your own rhythm, in your own time.

Invitation:
What does rising look like in this season for me?

September 25

Root into Daily Rituals

Rituals are roots. They stabilize you. Let your
mornings and evenings hold space for what matters.

Invitation:
What daily ritual can help me feel more grounded and present?

September 26

Let Roots Grow Deep

The deeper your roots, the stronger your rise. Focus inward. Grow beneath the surface.

Invitation:
Where in my life do I need deeper grounding?

September 27

Rise with Integrity

Let your growth be whole, not rushed. Rise with
values intact and soul in alignment.

Invitation:
What does rising with integrity mean for me right now?

September 28

The Softness of Completion

There is a moment near the end of every season when
you realize the work is already done.
Not because every detail is perfect, but because your
heart no longer resists what is ready to rest.
Completion isn't about finishing; it's about allowing.
It's the quiet confidence that what's unfolding no
longer needs your control — only your grace.

Invitation:
*Where can you release the need to finish and simply honor what
feels complete?*

September 29

The Pause Between

Today is the space between what has been and what is
coming.
It's the hush before the overture begins again — the
sacred stillness where wisdom gathers.
When you stop rushing to define the next chapter, life
reveals its own rhythm.
This is where alignment is born: not in movement, but
in listening.

Invitation:
*Can you let the pause be enough, trusting that clarity is already
finding you?*

September 30

Becoming Light Again

As this month closes, exhale what no longer belongs.
You are not who you were when September began.
You've softened, surrendered, and seen what remains true.
What stays now is only what your soul can carry with ease.
This is the grace of becoming — lighter, clearer, more whole.

Invitation:
*What truth are you ready to carry forward — and what will
you leave to grace?*

OCTOBER

OCTOBER

Grace Practice: The Beauty of Release

Collect leaves or write down old patterns, doubts, or
fears. One per day.
At week's end, burn or bury them with this blessing:
*"You once served me, now I set you free. I am not what I
release—I am what I reclaim."*

October 1

You're Still Becoming

You don't need to be finished to be beautiful. Celebrate
your in-process self.

Invitation:
What part of me is still becoming—and how can I honor her?

October 2

Growth Isn't Always Loud

Some seasons of growth are quiet. Subtle. Hidden. But
they matter just as much.

Invitation:
What quiet growth is happening in me right now?

October 3

Let Go of the Timeline

There's no rush. Your path unfolds on soul time, not societal time.

Invitation:
What timeline pressure can I release today?

October 4

Your Becoming is Sacred

Becoming is not a means to an end. It's the holy work
of being fully alive.

Invitation:
How can I honor my becoming as sacred today?

October 5

Trust the Layers

Every version of you had purpose. Every layer matters.
Trust the process.

Invitation:
What version of myself do I want to thank and release?

October 6

Becoming Requires Boundaries

To become who you are, you must protect your
becoming. Boundaries are love in action.

Invitation:
What boundary do I need to set to protect who I'm becoming?

October 7

You're Allowed to Change

Change doesn't make you inconsistent—it makes you real. Let your evolution speak.

Invitation:
Where am I being invited to evolve?

October 8

Simple is Sacred

The soul doesn't crave more—it craves meaning. Strip
it down. Return to what matters.

Invitation:
What would it look like to simplify with intention this week?

October 9

Clear the Clutter

Declutter your schedule, your home, your heart. Make
room for what restores.

Invitation:
What clutter—physical or emotional—can I release today?

October 10

Breathe Space Into Your Life

Busy is not a badge. Breathe. Leave space between the
notes of your life.

Invitation:
Where do I need more spaciousness?

October 11

Find Beauty in the Ordinary

There is holiness in the everyday. The warm cup. The clean sheets. The golden leaves. Notice it.

Invitation:
What ordinary moment felt beautiful today?

October 12

Say No to Make Room for Yes

Simplicity requires discernment. Each no is a sacred
yes to something deeper.

Invitation:
*What do I need to say no to in order to honor
what matters most?*

October 13

Return to the Essentials

You already know what matters most.
Come back to it.

Invitation:
What are my essentials—and how can I center them this week?

October 14

Live Lightly

Let today be light. Light on pressure. Light on judgment. Light in spirit.

Invitation:
What would it look like to live more lightly today?

October 15

Look Within

The most meaningful harvest is internal. Your insight,
healing, and growth are worth honoring.

Invitation:
What part of my inner journey deserves celebration today?

October 16

Count What Can't Be Measured

Not all abundance is visible. Peace, clarity, and emotional resilience are part of your harvest too.

Invitation:
What invisible gifts have I received this season?

October 17

You've Come So Far

Take a breath. Look back with gentle eyes. You've moved mountains, even if they were quiet ones.

Invitation:
What milestone have I reached that I haven't acknowledged?

October 18

Hold Gratitude Like Gold

Gratitude turns ordinary days into sacred ones. Let it become your lens.

Invitation:
What can I give deep thanks for today?

October 19

Receive Your Own Love

You've shown up, healed, held space, and grown. Let yourself receive that love, too.

Invitation:
How can I receive and appreciate my own efforts today?

October 20

Reflect with Reverence

Reflection isn't just looking back—it's bowing to the path that's shaped you.

Invitation:
What chapter of my story am I ready to honor with reverence?

October 21

Celebrate Quiet Strength

There's strength in the quiet, steady work you've done. Celebrate it—not just the outcome, but the endurance.

Invitation:
Where in my life have I shown quiet strength?

October 22

Belonging Begins Within

Belonging isn't about fitting in—it's about being true.
Start by belonging to yourself.

Invitation:
Where in my life am I craving deeper belonging?

October 23

Let Yourself Be Seen

True belonging happens when we show up as we are.
Be brave enough to be visible.

Invitation:
What part of me have I been hiding that's ready to be seen?

October 24

Worthiness Isn't Earned

You don't have to prove your worth to belong. You are already enough.

Invitation:
What would change if I truly believed I was worthy as I am?

October 25

Connect with Compassion

Compassion builds bridges. Offer it to yourself, then
to others. That's where belonging grows.

Invitation:
How can I lead with compassion in my connections today?

October 26

Find Your People

Your people will recognize your light. Go where you're
celebrated, not tolerated.

Invitation:
Who helps me feel most at home in myself?

October 27

You're Not Alone

Even in solitude, you are not alone. The world holds you. Your spirit supports you. You belong.

Invitation:
How can I feel more connected to something greater today?

October 28

Belonging Is a Practice

Belonging is nurtured, not found. Keep practicing—
by showing up, speaking up, and loving fully.

Invitation:
*What small action can I take today to deepen my sense of
belonging?*

October 29

Life Moves in Seasons

Like nature, your life has rhythms—times of blooming, resting, shedding. Let yourself move with the flow.

Invitation:
What season am I in—and how can I honor it?

October 30

The Wisdom in Waiting

Sometimes waiting is not a pause, but a preparation.
Trust what's ripening beneath the surface.

Invitation:
What is quietly preparing to emerge in my life?

October 31

Endings Make Space

Let this final day of October be a soft ending. Make space for what's next by blessing what has been.

Invitation:
What can I release today to create space for my next beginning?

NOVEMBER

NOVEMBER

Deepening into Grace

Let November be a month of rooted stillness and soul-deep reflection. As the days grow shorter, let yourself turn inward and gather the wisdom of what has been. This is a time to listen to your intuition, reconnect with your inner light, and move with steady grace toward what's most essential.

Each day, name one moment that made your heart softer, not just happier.
Write it down with this phrase:

"Because of this, I remember who I am."

By month's end, you'll hold a sacred story of your truest self.

November 1

The Pause Has Purpose

Stillness isn't empty—it's full of knowing. Let yourself
pause without guilt.

Invitation:
Where can I welcome stillness as a gift today?

November 2

Listen to the Quiet

Beneath the noise is your truth. Listen in. Let silence
speak.

Invitation:
What is the quiet within me trying to say?

November 3

Do Less, Be More

Your worth isn't in how much you do. It's in who you
are when all else falls away.

Invitation:
What would it look like to be instead of do?

November 4

Settle Into Yourself

Let this day be gentle. Let it be soft. Let yourself settle
back into your own skin.

Invitation:
What helps me feel safe and at home in myself?

November 5

Sacred Slowness

Let life be slow today. Walk slower. Breathe deeper.
Speak with intention.

Invitation:
What pace honors my energy today?

November 6

Unplug to Reconnect

Take a break from screens, from noise, from rush.
Reconnect with your own rhythm.

Invitation:
What space can I create by unplugging?

November 7

Be Held by the Stillness

Let the stillness hold you like a mother. Let it soften
what's hard and calm what's loud.

Invitation:
How can I let stillness nurture me today?

November 8

Let Gratitude Lead

Gratitude isn't just a feeling—it's a lens. Let it guide how you move through the day.

Invitation:
What can I appreciate about this exact moment?

November 9

Say Thank You for the Hard Things

Gratitude expands when we can find it in the
challenge, the stretch, the growth.

Invitation:
What difficult experience taught me something valuable?

November 10

Small Thanks, Big Shift

A whispered thank you for morning light, warm tea, a kind word—these moments shift everything.

Invitation:
What small blessing can I name right now?

November 11

Gratitude Softens the Heart

Let thankfulness melt resentment. Let it open space
for healing and joy.

Invitation:
Where can gratitude help me soften today?

November 12

Be Grateful for Yourself

You've shown up again and again. Honor the you that's
still standing.

Invitation:
What am I proud of myself for, and how can I give thanks for it?

November 13

Let Gratitude Be Contagious

Your gratitude affects those around you. Let your
thankfulness ripple outward.

Invitation:
Who do I want to express gratitude to today?

November 14

Make Gratitude a Ritual

Let it be how you begin and end your day. Let it be
how you return to joy.

Invitation:
What gratitude ritual can I create to anchor my days?

November 15

Your Light Is Needed

Even on hard days, your presence carries light. Don't
underestimate your impact.

Invitation:
Where am I being called to bring light today?

November 16

Refuel Your Flame

Your light needs tending. Rest, beauty, laughter, solitude—these are matches for your soul.

Invitation:
What helps refuel my inner light?

November 17

Let Yourself Shine

Stop shrinking. Your light isn't too much—it's
medicine for someone else's shadow.

Invitation:
What part of my brilliance am I ready to let shine?

November 18

Guard Your Glow

Protect your peace. Not everyone deserves access to
your inner fire.

Invitation:
What boundary will help preserve my inner light?

November 19

Light Can Be Gentle

Your light doesn't need to be loud. It can be soft and still sacred.

Invitation:
How can I let my light be present in quiet ways?

November 20

Shine in Your Own Way

You don't need to shine like anyone else. Authentic
light is never a copy.

Invitation:
What does it look like when I shine as only I can?

November 21

Illuminate From Within

External validation fades. Let your light rise from the
inside out.

Invitation:
What helps me stay connected to my internal glow?

November 22

Abundance Begins Within

True abundance isn't about accumulation—it's about
deep presence and appreciation.

Invitation:
Where in my life do I already have more than enough?

November 23

Give Thanks in Layers

Peel back the surface and give thanks for the deep,
layered gifts—your growth, your resilience, your hope.

Invitation:
What layered blessing am I grateful for today?

November 24

Celebrate What Money Can't Buy

Love, laughter, connection, peace. These are the riches
that make life full.

Invitation:
What non-material abundance fills my life?

November 25

Be Generous With Your Light

Give what you want to receive—love, encouragement,
grace. You are a wellspring.

Invitation:
*What can I give freely today that costs nothing but means
everything?*

November 26

Remember the Source

Return to the Source that fills you—Spirit, Earth,
Love. Anchor into what sustains your soul.

Invitation:
What or who is the source of my abundance?

November 27

Abundance Grows When Shared

The more you share, the more it expands. Let your life
become a blessing to others.

Invitation:
Where can I share my abundance today?

November 28

Be Abundance

You don't just receive abundance—you *are* abundance.
Walk as if the universe lives in you.

Invitation:
What does it feel like to embody abundance?

November 29

Welcome the Turn

As seasons shift, let yourself shift too. Change doesn't
erase you—it reveals you.

Invitation:
What change am I ready to meet with grace?

November 30

Close the Month with Intention

Before stepping into what's next, pause. Name what you've lived. Bless what's behind you.

Invitation:
What do I want to carry forward—and what can I leave behind?

DECEMBER

DECEMBER

A Season of Inner Light

December asks us to slow down, light the fire within, and gather what is sacred. It is the season of deep listening, of soulful reflection, and of soft hope. Let these final weeks of the year anchor you in wisdom, wonder, and gentle courage.

Each evening, light a candle and whisper this prayer:

"May I carry what matters. May I release what weighs. May I be at peace in the waiting."

Sit for five minutes with the flame. Let the light hold what words cannot.

December 1

Carry Your Own Light

The days grow short, but your soul still shines. Let
your inner light lead the way.

Invitation:
How can I be my own source of light today?

December 2

What You Illuminate Matters

Shine light on what matters—truth, kindness, healing, joy. Let your focus bring it to life.

Invitation:
What do I want to illuminate through my presence?

December 3

Tend the Spark

Your light doesn't have to be blazing. A spark is
enough. Tend it. Protect it.

Invitation:
What small practice helps me keep my light alive?

December 4

Shine for Someone Else

Sometimes your light helps another find their way. Be
a gentle lantern today.

Invitation:
Who might need my light, and how can I offer it with grace?

December 5

Embrace the Darkness Too

There is wisdom in the dark. Let it teach you. Let it hold you.

Invitation:
What might the darkness be inviting me to see?

December 6

Let the Light Find You

You don't have to chase the light. Be still. Let it rise
from within.

Invitation:
What brings me back to my center when life feels dim?

December 7

Shine Without Shame

You don't have to dim to belong. Let your light be
holy, honest, and whole.

Invitation:
What light within me have I been afraid to share?

December 8

Permission to Be New

There comes a moment when the woman you've been can no longer carry the woman you're becoming.
This is not failure — it's evolution.

Winter invites you to release the version of yourself that survived...
so you can finally meet the one who is ready to live.

Let today be the day you whisper yes to the parts of you that long to rise.
You don't need a full plan.
Just permission.
Just breath.
Just willingness.

Invitation:
What part of me is ready to become new, even if I can't see the whole path yet?

December 9

Rest is a Strategy

The world glorifies exhaustion, but your body
recognizes truth before your mind does.
When you slow down, clarity can catch up to you.

Rest is not a reward — it is a strategy.
A woman who knows how to restore herself is a
woman who moves with precision.

Allow yourself a quieter pace today.
Your worth is not measured in motion.

Invitation:
Where have I been pushing when I'm actually being called to restore?

December 10

What You Lay Down Matters

Winter teaches us that release is sacred.
Not everything is meant to travel with you into your
next season — not every habit, not every fear, not
every expectation.

Let this day be an invitation to set something down.
Not because you're giving up, but because you're
choosing to carry only what is aligned.

Invitation:
What am I ready to lay down so I can rise with more intention?

December 11

The Quiet Truth

There is a truth inside you — small, steady,
unshakeable.
It doesn't shout.
It doesn't argue.
It doesn't negotiate.
It simply waits for you to get quiet enough to hear it
again.
Today, trust the truth that arrives in stillness.
Truth spoken gently is still truth.

Invitation:
What quiet truth is whispering to me right now?

December 12

Grace for the Middle

Transformation rarely happens in the dramatic
moments.
It happens on days like this —
the middle days,
the in-between days,
the days when nothing looks remarkable…
but something inside is shifting.

Give yourself grace for the middle.
This is where your roots strengthen.

Invitation:
What small, unseen shift is happening within me right now?

December 13

You Are Not Behind

There is no timeline you must obey.
No comparison you must outrun.
No standard you must prove.

You are not behind.
You are becoming — and becoming has its own
rhythm, its own pace, its own holy timing.

Trust that your life is right on time.

Invitation:
Where have I been judging my pace,
and what would trust look like instead?

December 14

The Light Returns Slowly

Even in the deepest part of winter, the light is already
returning — quietly, incrementally, faithfully.
Your clarity works the same way.

You do not need a spotlight to move forward.
A single glimmer is enough.
A small warm knowing is enough.
A breath of ease is enough.

Let the slow returning be sufficient.

Invitation:
What small light within me is beginning to return?

December 15

Let Hope Be Gentle

Hope doesn't have to be loud. Sometimes it's a quiet
flicker that keeps you moving forward.

Invitation:
Where do I feel a quiet hope rising in me?

December 16

Hope After the Storm

Even after hard seasons, hope still finds you. Let it
arrive softly, like morning light.

Invitation:
*What hardship have I walked through that now makes room for
hope?*

December 17

Choose Hope on Purpose

Hope isn't naïve—it's courageous. Choose it. Practice
it. Let it guide you.

Invitation:
What would choosing hope look like today?

December 18

Anchor Your Hope

Tie your hope to something strong—love, purpose,
faith. Let it root deep.

Invitation:
What anchors my hope when I feel unsteady?

December 19

Hope in the Ordinary

Hope hides in the simplest places—in a laugh, a
sunrise, a deep breath. Notice it.

Invitation:
Where did I encounter hope in an ordinary moment?

December 20

Share Your Hope

Someone else needs your hope to believe in their own.
Offer it freely.

Invitation:
How can I extend hope to someone else today?

December 21

Hope is a Light You Carry

Hope isn't something you wait for—it's something you hold. Let it shine.

Invitation:
What hope will I carry into the rest of this season?

WINTER

The Inner Sanctuary

Winter whispers rest. It is the season where your soul curls inward, seeking quiet and stillness.

Let this time be your sacred cocoon, a holy pause from the pace of becoming.

You are allowed to be undone and unhurried. You are allowed to nest and nourish, to be with yourself fully.

In the hush of winter, you are reminded: you don't have to bloom to be beautiful. You are already worthy in the waiting.

December 22

Completion, Not Perfection

You don't need to finish perfectly—you only need to arrive whole. Let completion be enough.

Invitation:
What am I proud to have carried through to completion?

December 23

Rest in Your Becoming

You have become so much more than you imagined.
Rest in that truth today.

Invitation:
How have I changed in ways that truly matter?

December 24

Let Joy Be Simple

Joy doesn't need to be big or loud. Let it come in quiet
forms—presence, peace, stillness.

Invitation:
Where can I find joy in simplicity today?

December 25

A Day of Sacred Celebration

Whether surrounded or still, let this day be sacred.
Celebrate the light within and around you.

Invitation:
What can I celebrate in myself and my life today?

December 26

Hold What Matters

Release the pressure. Hold what matters—love, breath,
presence, peace.

Invitation:
What really matters to me right now, and how can I honor it?

December 27

Soft Strength

Let softness be your strength today. Gentleness is not
weakness—it is resilience refined.

Invitation:
Where can I lead with soft strength?

December 28

You Are the Miracle

You don't need to do more, prove more, or earn more.
You are the miracle. Just as you are.

Invitation:
What would change if I truly believed I am already enough?

December 29

Welcome What's Next

Let go of fear about the future. What's ahead holds possibility, beauty, and bold beginnings.

Invitation:
How can I meet the new year with openness?

December 30

Make Peace With the Past

Forgive. Release. Bless it all. You don't need to carry
what no longer serves.

Invitation:
What am I ready to forgive and release before the year ends?

December 31

Rise With Intention

Don't just cross the finish line—rise with vision. Step into the next season with clarity and grace.

Invitation:
Who do I want to become in the new year?

YEAR-END REFLECTION

List your top 5 soul shifts, 3 hardest lessons, and 3 most sacred wins of the year. Honor it all. You've lived, loved, grown, and risen.

Write a vision for your next chapter. Begin with: *"In this new season, I will rise by..."* Let this be your soul's resolution.

A CLOSING NOTE

You didn't just finish a book.

You moved through a year of your life—one moment at a time, one choice at a time. You made space for truth. You chose intention over performance. You reconnected with the strength that was always yours.

This isn't an ending. It's a confirmation.

You are ready for what comes next—not because everything is certain, but because you are aligned with what matters.

Let grace stay with you.

In your decisions. In your boundaries. In the way you lead, speak, rest, and rise.

You were never meant to stay the same. You were meant to live awake—to the woman you've become, and to the life you now claim as your own.

This is your life. Lead it with grace.